COLLECTOR'S ENCYCLOPEDIA OF

Lefton CHINA

Loretta DeLozier

COLLECTOR BOOKS
A Division of Schroeder Publishing Co., Inc.

Searching for a Publisher?

We are always looking for knowledgeable people considered to be experts within their fields. If you feel that there is a real need for a book on your collectible subject and have a large comprehensive collection, contact us.

COLLECTOR BOOKS
P.O. Box 3009
Paducah, Kentucky 42002-3009

Cover design: Beth Summers
Book design: Pamela Shumaker

On cover: 14" x 8½" Coach with two horses.

Excerpts from brochures published by the Geo. Zoltan Lefton Company are included in this volume. Also the trademarks #6, #8, and #12 are the registered trademarks of Geo. Zoltan Lefton Company and the trademarks #1, #2, #3, #4, #5, #7, #9, #10, and #11 are the trademarks of Geo. Zoltan Lefton Company. Certain photographs, reprinted by permission of the Geo. Zoltan Company, are by Carl Knize and Marlene Binkley, Lefton's Photographers and were taken in 1993.

Additional copies of this book may be ordered from:

Collector Books
P.O. Box 3009
Paducah, KY 42002-3009
or
Loretta DeLozier
1101 Polk St.
Bedford, IA 50833

@$19.95. Add $2.00 for postage and handling.
Copyright: Loretta DeLozier, 1995

Dedication

This book is dedicated to my wonderful husband and friend, Jim DeLozier. His patience with me after hours of searching through antique shops, antique malls, shows, markets, and all the various places a person searches for Lefton, his encouragement, and all his hard work will never be forgotten. He has helped me with his ideas and suggestions as well as materials and pictures. Without his total love, loyalty, and devotion this price guide would not have been possible.

Acknowledgments

This book has been made possible by those people who have so willingly given information about their collections.

I am especially thankful to Ed Jalloway for the pictures of his collection along with his encouragement and help with many items. Merrill and Lois Struck, Rich and Alma Rogers, Dorie Kwarcinski and many others for pictures, knowledge and help. To Rebecca Sult for her special efforts in the photographing of certian pieces. A special thanks to Nancy Rahn for her enthusiasm and for putting me in touch with the right people to accomplish this finished product. Last, but by far not the least, The Lefton China Company and the complete Lefton staff for their cooperation.

Photographs in this volume have been made available as follows:

1. The official Lefton photographers, Carl Knize and Marlene Binkley, provided the author with some photographs of Lefton marks and pieces.
2. Some photographs have been made by individual collectors for which the author has obtained appropriate releases.
3. Some photographs of Lefton pieces have been taken by the husband of the author from collections of individuals for which the author has obtained appropriate releases.
4. The balance of the photographs have been taken from the collection of the author.

ontents

Preface

When the Lefton people recognized that their products were becoming collectibles they attempted to stay clear of any association with the secondary market but, were forced by the pressures from that marketplace to provide a limited degree of background data on their company, their products, and the system of marks and labels used to identify the individual pieces and the approximate dates they were produced. The Geo. Zoltan Lefton Company is to be commended for the strong position they took to avoid a conflict of interest between the secondary market and their current, very active involvement in the manufacturing and marketing of china. Positive relationships of the cost of manufacturing, marketing, shipping, and handling directly forecast the selling price of an item. But, the intangible value that that can be placed on a collectible, and for the many, many reasons people elect to collect them, makes the price of a collectible extremely difficult to establish.

I have been involved with Lefton for only a few short years. Like most of you interested in Lefton, I kept asking the questions, "Where can I get some information on Lefton? Has there been a book written?" My questions and interest brought about a suggestion from a book store operator that I write the book myself. My initial efforts made *Schroeder's Antiques Price Guide* with only 20 of the many thousands of Lefton pieces manufactured. This encouraged me to go one step further and direct my energies to writing a price guide to help others like me. Naturally, such an undertaking required help from the Lefton Company. They were most understanding and cooperative and I'm sure they saw me as just another inquirer that would soon go away. The more I learned, the more my interest grew, and the more information I needed. Finally, after a visit to the comapny's office and lunch with Mr. Lefton (this reference always implies Mr. George Zoltan Lefton) things very slowly started to happen.

On that same visit Mr. John Lefton made the casual comment that "I was for real." You can imagine how this produced even greater incentive and enthusiasm that ultimately led me to receiving absolute cooperation from the entire Lefton staff. I found it to be a sincere honor and privilege to be handed boxes of records, permitting me to document much of the history of Lefton China.

However, like most other things in life, the more you know simply tells you how very much you don't know. Unfortunately, Lefton never planned for a collectible market and failed to develop an infallible record keeping or product identification system, making the job of record searching a real challenge. Only with the continued cordial help of the Lefton people did I have the opportunity to review old files and talk to those individuals who still remembered the history of a certain item or a mark and detailed manufacturing information.

It is obvious that Lefton has been cooperative in my venture but what may not be apparent is the help obtained from the collectors. A few of these most deserving people have been indentified in the Acknowledgments of this guide. There were many more who allowed me to take pictures and question them about their collecitons. I have found that Lefton collectors symbolize the beauty and quality of the Lefton China they collect.

I cannot overemphasize the fact that the Lefton family has made it abundantly clear that they wish to maintain an arm's length in pricing any previously manufactured items. My interest and sincerity was apparent to them and only by assuring Lefton that my price guide would be of the type fitting the quality of their product was their cooperation granted and did this book become a reality.

The Birth of a Collectible

Everything in nature and everything made by man can and will be collected by someone at some time. A simple but true statement. Rocks, shells, butterflies, and fossils are but a few of the "natural" items collected. Stamps, sports cards, paintings, tools, marbles, and of course china are but a few of the man-made collectibles. However, of all the many and diverse items that people collect, I feel that those of beauty are the most deserving. Lefton China certainly fits that category.

When items hit the marketplace, from a manufacturer with a prior history known for products that increase in value, they are snatched up and collected for resale or trading at a later date. The scarcity of a limited edition may be an instant bonanza. These events don't go unnoticed and may encourage the collecting instincts in people. What triggers the regional, national, or international collection of any one thing? We do. People like you and me, through acquisition, resale, conversations, displays, and advertisements.

Mr. Lefton's efforts and imagination in china have been for the entire home, not just the dining room. As a result the name Lefton will be immortalized and has joined the other great names in decorative china. The difference being that Mr. Lefton is a man of our times. Someone that has been part of the U.S. history, during the age of atomic energy and desk top computers, and someone who placed quality above price, beauty above marketing, and business ethics above personal success.

Loretta DeLozier and George Zoltan Lefton

History of Lefton China

Everyone that writes any type of history should make a sincere effort to be concise and accurate. However, much of history occurs with little or no written documentation. Revisiting the events that make history often permits an author to add a little personal flavor and thoughts that could distort the facts, so no one is really sure what is fact or fiction. So in the case of this historical record of Lefton China you will either have to trust me or do your own research to refute the information I have for you. I can only assure you that what you are about to read is an honest account of the founding of a long-to-be-remembered china importing and marketing organization.

Lefton China is the brainchild of George Zoltan Lefton. Hungarian born and bred but with a conception of business as much like an American as Henry Ford or John Rockefeller. You don't have to build cars or strike oil to see a marketing opportunity and Mr. Lefton simply found gold along the streets of Chicago. It wasn't gushing from the ground or smelted in a furnace, it was by creating a beautiful product that would be cherished by thousands, even millions of people, for the present and for the future.

Lefton's own written historical description begins simply as:

"In the mid-1930's George Zoltan Lefton, a native of Hungary, was earning a living by designing and manufacturing sportswear. As a hobby, he collected fine porcelain. Seeking freedom and opportunity, Lefton set sail for America in 1939. He arrived in Chicago and his passion for collecting porcelain began to shape ideas for a new business. By early 1941, Lefton's desire for quality ceramics overpowered any feelings he might have had for fabric and fashion, so he created his own ceramics business.

At the conclusion of World War II, he saw the opportunities for reviving the Oriental skills in porcelain and importing them for the American consumer. It wasn't long before he found himself deeply planted in the industry, importing giftware from the Orient and being unofficially known as "The China King." Today, the company is the leading producer of ceramic giftware and its products are found in gift shops around the world."

Though this little bit of rhetoric meets my criteria for expressing history — concise and accurate, it does leave out events that made Mr. Lefton's efforts unique in the porcelain industry.

In between the first and second paragraph of that brief history occured America's involvement in World War II, beginning on Sunday morning, December 7, 1941. When that historical event became known in Chicago it was early Sunday afternoon. While at his business, Mr. Lefton had a friend and business neighbor whom he valued as one of his own relatives. Upon hearing of the Japanese attack on Pearl Harbor, and without any fanfare, he began to purchase lumber, locate ladders, hammers, and nails, and proceeded to board up the unprotected glass front of his friend's business. This was done not a minute to soon. Almost "gang like" Chicago residents were moving through the street, identifying Japanese citizens, threatening bodily harm and destroying every Japanese owned business they could reach until law and order was restored. You see, Mr. Lefton's friend and business neighbor was a Japanese-American.

This same friend played an important role in Mr. Lefton's selection of Japan as his major manufacturing source for items which have that familiar Lefton paper label or the various fired on marks. (Some common and some extremely rare.)

Lefton added more Japanese and other Oriental manufacturers to its list of suppliers over the next 40 years. However, until just recently, the majority of the items it marketed originated from Japanese sources. With Lefton's continuation of quality specifications for its hand picked suppliers, items marketed today will be in demand long into the future.

Lefton Factories

Historically, the principal source of Lefton China was factories in Japan. In the mid 1970's the circumstances changed with regard to sources in Japan that apparently caused Lefton to seek factories and porcelain suppliers from other Oriental locations. Taiwan, Malaysia, and China, among others, have been added as principal sources as their factory quality and performance proved to meet Lefton's strict requirements. However, the majority of items sold by Lefton that are included in this price guide, and now found in the secondary marketplace, were manufactured in Japan.

Though many different factories were used to satisfy the high volume marketing ability of Lefton, the same or a very similar procedure was employed to introduce each piece to its customers.

The creation of most every item of Lefton China began with a marketing idea. This was translated to a designer who perfected that idea into a sketch sufficient for a sculptor to mold and shape it into a three dimensional model. Once that shape was approved, a trial mold was made from which a new prototype was produced. If it proved to be satisfactory, a master mold was made of quality materials that permitted it to turn out many production molds. From the master mold a sufficient number of production molds were made to satisfy the total production run, knowing a production mold could probably produce only 25 to 30 quality items.

The items of the production run were fired, decorations and painting added, then the item was refired. A few of the more intricate items may even require three or more firings to provide the desired finish. Delicate leaves and flower petals were hand shaped from a ball of clay by a tool similar to a carver's gouge or they may have been molded in a simple cut out mold, shaped by that same type tool, and carefully attached by hand or tweezers to the item. An assembly line technique was employed by many factories and production rates of 5,000 to 50,000 or more per month were commonplace depending on the capability of the factory and the strict specifications or the delicateness of the item.

The quality standards of Lefton were well known to all factories that produced items for them. The fact that there were hundreds, if not thousands, of ceramic factories to choose from and Lefton being one of their better customers, makes it easy to see how Lefton managed to maintain its high level of quality control over the years. If quality fell below standard, the factories that Lefton dealt with would take the items back or authorized their destruction and replaced them with acceptable ones.

As a new collector of Lefton you may have to turn a piece upside down to know for sure that it is Lefton. Later, as your eye becomes sharper, you will be nearly certain of the outcome before you turn the item over. This is what I call "The Lefton Difference."

Marks

Not unlike other porcelain importing and marketing companies, Lefton's beginning placed little emphasize on developing a system for dating their products. Fortunately; however, a system did emerge that does help the collector.

Rather than use a standard mark, created by the Lefton Company, the style, color, and type of mark was often left up to the porcelain manufacturer. The Lefton Company references, as we know them today, began just after World War II, however; from 1940 to 1946 there may have been Lefton China that Mr. Lefton purchased and sold, but little is known about the marks that were used. Universal Statues made products for Mr. Lefton to sell domestically but my research has not uncovered any type of identification that would help the collector. The items made between 1945 and 1953 were labeled "Made in Occupied Japan," as was required by law during General MacArthur's administration of post-war Japan.

Most Lefton items are identified by a fired on trademark or a paper label located on the bottom of the piece. Also some pieces, made in the 1950's and later years, had the year of copyright placed below the trademark, but usually any number found there is the item identification number. Certain registered and unregistered trademarks and logos of Geo. Zoltan Lefton Company have been appropriately credited. If the number is preceded by letters, these will be the abbreviated factory identification. Trademarks are found in both single color and multicolor styles. A few of the factory identifications are shown below and some of the marks used are pictured on the following pages. The marks and their official dates of manufacture, according to the Lefton Company, are shown on page 11.*

SL - Nippon Art China K.K.	KF - Kobayashi Toki K.K.
SF - G.K. Shimizu Toen Seitosho	PY - Miyao Toki K.K.
YX - Yada Toki K.K.	KW - Kowa Toki K.K.
C - K.K. Seiyei	YK - Yamakuni Seito K.K.
RH - Bito	CY - Chubu Yogyo K.K.
YS - Yamagata Seitosho	NE - Endo Toki K.K.
WK - Wako Toki K.K.	YU - Yamamoto Seito Y.K.

Though there are many identification numbers that bear the same factory identification letters, this guide has avoided the use of most factory prefaces and used only the numbers that would have appeared in the original Lefton inventory records and catalogs. You may find that there was more than one factory that would produce the same item and more than one item that could bear the same number. Confusing? Of course it is. This is the reason that it will take the number and the description to match to be certain you are talking about the same piece.

To add a little more to your knowledge of the numbering system, you will find suffix letters that are reasonably easy to explain. "R" may mean "rose," "V" may mean "violet," "S" may mean "small," "L" may mean "large" but then "R" can mean "right" and "L" can mean "left." To an informed collector, many other clues for identificaiton will surely present themselves.

*Excerpts from brochure published by the Geo. Zoltan Lefton Company.

LEFTON TRADEMARKS UPDATE

1946 – 1950
(1)

LAMORE CHINA ENTIRELY HANDMADE G.Z.L. U.S.A. MADE IN JAPAN

1946 – 1950
(2)

MADE IN OCCUPIED JAPAN

1948 – 1953
(3)

MADE IN JAPAN

1948 – 1953
(4)

1950 – 1955
(5)

1949 – 1955
(6)

1950 – 1955
(7)

1948 – 1953
(8)

MADE IN JAPAN

1955 – PRESENT
(9)

1955 – PRESENT
(10)

1977 – PRESENT
(11)

FROM 1982
(12)

"The trademarks #6, #8 and #12 are the registered trademarks of Geo. Zoltan Lefton Company, and the trademarks #1, #2, #3, #4, #5, #7, #9, #10, and #11 are the trademarks of Geo. Zoltan Lefton Company." Brochure from Lefton Co. *A Guide to Collecting, Second Edition.*

General Information

There are a lot of subtle little hints that I have learned from my field searches for Lefton that may be helpful to the novice or beginner Lefton collector. Though I have no real way of guaranteeing this information, it has proven successful for me and I hope it will add to your pleasure of the hunt.

Many of the Lefton items were manufactured in two or more sizes, many different colors, designs, and styles. It is really hard to believe just how many items are out there. Tableware came in full sets from plates, cups, saucers, bowls, and other major pieces down to butter pats, salt and pepper shakers, and demitasse. I've found the dinner plates and salad plates of these sets to be quite difficult to locate, maybe because they are still in use, or in the case of other flatware, were simply used every day and did not fair well.

Like any painted, dyed, or stained item of furniture or houseware, colors are never 100% consistent. You must always select from the same "run" of carpet or drapery to be assured of uniform color. This is also true of porcelain and is even more of a problem when a high firing temperature can greatly distort any color. Therefore, look for uniform color in a series but don't turn something down just because of a slight color difference. Though maybe not from the same "run" it could be from the same mold.

Many Lefton items were marketed with marks, identification numbers, and paper labels. Some were sold with only one of the three. It is easy to see that the paper labels could wear or wash off. The resale value will be understandably higher if all the usual identification is present, but until you become more familiar with the Lefton look of quality and appearance, you can be safe by buying from trademark or label only.

An interesting point my research has uncovered is the fact that a specific number can represent two or more very different items. You will find letter prefixes sometimes help solve this problem, but don't be surprised when your collector friend tells you they found an item by number that turns out to be something different than you expected. When communicating with dealers and collectors I think you will find it important to describe the article by size, shape, color, trademark, decorations, and number, if available.

Pricing a Collectible

The majority of collectors purchase from the normal sources — antique dealers and antique malls, with a few purchases made at auctions or from private collectors. Therefore, this guide is somewhat directed at the price the dealer would be asking the collector to pay.

Just how does a dealer create his original asking price? Price guides like this help. The dealer's own experience and comparable pricing add credence. The price the dealer paid for the item certainly dictates to some degree what he anticipates the resale value to be.

Limited edition or reduced quantity of a certain item *usually* adds to its value. I say usually because my opinion has been altered in developing values for Lefton China. My search of Lefton's historical records reflects a number of items maintained on inventory cards were often cancelled after a very limited number were purchased. This was not the result of purposely creating a limited edition, it was simply the result of production difficulties which made it very costly to produce. Sure, a very small quantity of those items was marketed with the Lefton trademark, but it appears that some of those items tend to remain undesirable while others grow rapidly in price. The reason for this I find difficult to explain.

I have had the opportunity to visit auctions, antique malls, antique dealers, and private collectors from coast to coast and strangely enough find prices to be relatively consistent. The latest pricing information seems to spread quickly across the nation. Fewer *good buys* are available as people cling to their Lefton collections.

Like all fine china, condition is a principal factor in the price. Unfortunately, the very thing that makes so many pieces of Lefton extremely desirable is the same thing that often caused a diminishing price. Most of the hand applied floral patterns are extremely delicate. Rather than having smooth, rounded edges, Lefton chose to design into many themes a thin and sharp edged configuration closely resembling the real thing. Therefore, it is difficult if not impossible to find perfect specimens of Lefton in their bisque series. However, my prices reflect values of items that are as close to being perfect as you can locate. Damaged pieces should be reduced in value as the purchaser perceives, remembering however, that you may have a long wait to find that perfect piece.

Furthermore, pricing and appraising is not a pure science. My prices will surely be challenged by some as too high and others as too low. However, I think my system has proven consistent and reflects the current real marketplace. Undoubtedly, this relatively new to the industry collectible will make rapid adjustments and corrections to its pricing structure and you can be sure that the second edition of this guide will stay abreast of these changes. There is no question in my mind that Lefton China is the developing giant in the collectible field and will surprise any critic that would think otherwise. The whole world is in a frenzy over collecting something and because one has the opportunity to collect Lefton in a wide variety of sets, series, themes, combinations, clusters, colors, and patterns makes it a collector's dream.

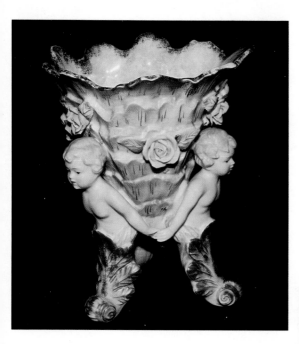

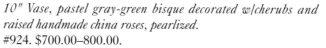
10" Vase, pastel gray-green bisque decorated w/cherubs and
raised handmade china roses, pearlized.
#924. $700.00–800.00.

7" Candy bowl in pastel green bisque finish w/fluted
gold edge, w/cherub decoration, pearlized.
#837. $120.00–140.00.

7" Angel on tree, pastel gray-green bisque finish, pair.
#953. $175.00–195.00.

5½" Basket, pastel colored bisque finish.
#964. $110.00–130.00.

9" x 7" Beautifully proportioned bowl in gray-green bisque w/2
cherubs decorated in gold on edge, and raised handmade pink roses.
#741. $400.00–500.00.

14" x 8½" Coach w/two horses, on cover.
#834. $1,200.00–1,400.00.

6¼" Cornucopia vases, gracefully shaped in pastel green bisque, dec-
orated with raised pink roses, pair.
#774. $85.00–95.00.

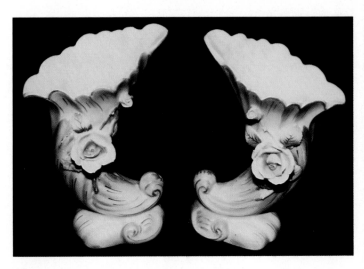

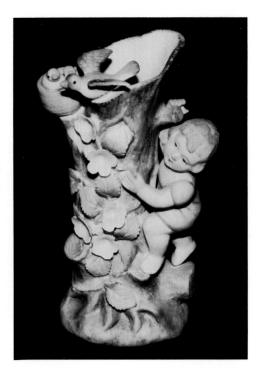

6½" Tree trunk vase, pastel gray-green bisque finish, pair.
#970. $110.00–120.00.

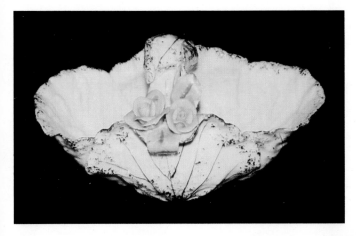

6" Leaf dish decorated in sponge gold and raised pink china roses.
#961. $47.00–52.00.

7½" White bisque Cornucopia vases
decorated w/pink roses, pair.
#672. $95.00–105.00.

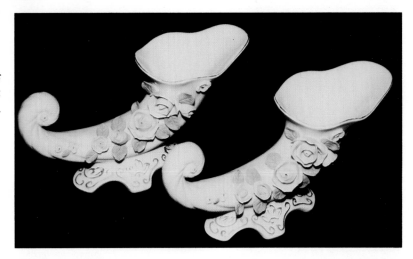

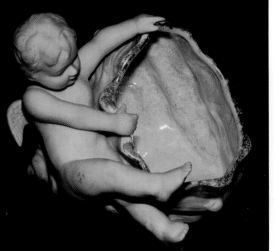

6" Shell bowl w/angel, gray-green pastel bisque finished, pearlized.
#825. $95.00–105.00.

Angels

4" Angel of the month, January, Febuary, March.
#3332. $25.00–30.00 each.

4" Angel of the month, April, May, June.
#3332. $25.00–30.00 each.

4" Angel of the month, July.
#3332. $25.00–30.00 .

4" Angel of the month, August, September, October.
#3332. $25.00–30.00 each.

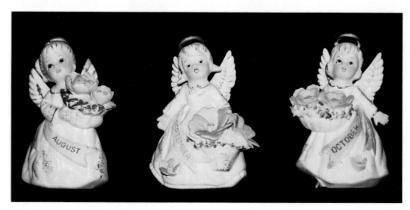

4" Angel of the month, November, December.
#3332. $25.00–30.00 each.

5" Flower girl of the month, January.
#985. $28.00–32.00.

5" Flower girl of the month, March.
#985. $28.00–32.00.

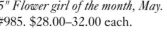

5" Flower girl of the month, May.
#985. $28.00–32.00 each.

5" Flower girl of the month, July.
#985. $28.00–32.00.

5" Flower girl of the month, September.
#985. $28.00–32.00.

5" Flower girl of the month, October.
#985. $28.00–32.00.

5" Flower girl of the month, November, December.
#985. $28.00–32.00 each.

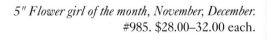

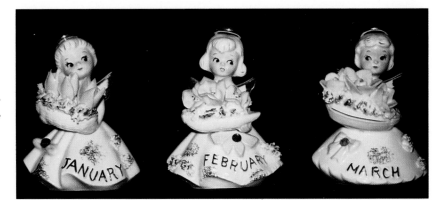

4" Angel of the month, January, February, March.
#489. $25.00-30.00 each.

4" Angel of the month, April, May, June.
#489. $25.00-30.00 each.

4" Angel of the month, July, September.
#489. $25.00-30.00 each.

4" Angel of the month, October, November, December.
#489. $25.00-30.00 each.

3½" Kissing angels.
#2079. $8.00–10.00.

4" Angel climber.
#389. $12.00–15.00.

3¼" x 4" Angel in frame, Monday.
#6883. $28.00–32.00.

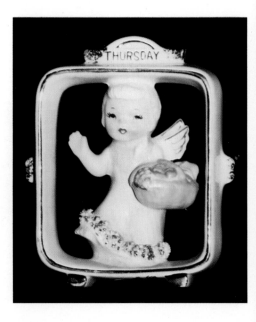

3¼" x 4" Angel in frame, Thursday.
#6883. $28.00–32.00.

3¼" x 4" Angel in frame, Friday.
#6883. $28.00–32.00.

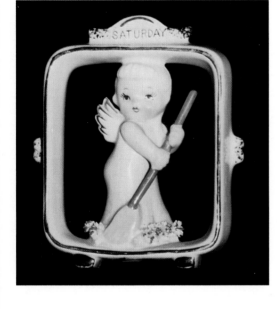

3¼" x 4" Angel in frame, Saturday.
#6883. $28.00–32.00.

3¼" x 4" Angel in frame, Sunday.
#6883. $28.00–32.00.

4" Angel of the week, named for each day, Saturday, Sunday.
#8281. $30.00–35.00.

4" Angel of the week, named for each day, Monday.
#8281. $30.00–35.00.

4" Angel of the week, named for each day, Tuesday.
#8281. $30.00–35.00.

4" Angel of the week, named for each day, Wednesday.
#8281. $30.00–35.00.

4" Angel of the week, named for each day, Thursday.
#8281. $30.00–35.00.

4" Angel of the week, named for each day, Friday.
#8281. $30.00–35.00.

5½" Boy angel of the month, March.
#556. $25.00–30.00.

4" Flower girl of the month.
#595. $25.00–30.00.

5" Angel of the week in round frame, Thursday.
#6949. $28.00–32.00.

Banks

5½" Pig, pearl luster.
#1122. $16.00–18.00.

5" Purse, pink.
#90256. $35.00–45.00.

6½" Owl, bisque.
#479. $21.00–26.00.

7½" Lady and man retirement.
#4293 & 4266. $15.00–18.00 each.

6½" Owl with rhinestone eyes.
#90195. $45.00–50.00.

6" Owl with glass eyes.
#3893. $10.00–12.00.

Birds and Animals

11¾" Golden pheasant.
#1060. $40.00–50.00.

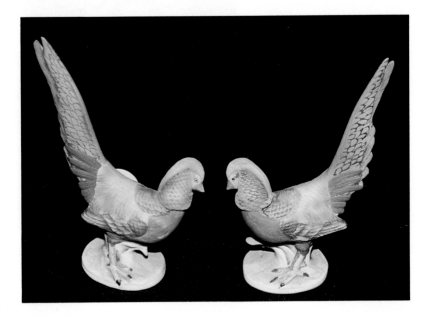

5½" Golden pheasant.
#1529. $30.00–35.00 pair.

8¼" Pheasant.
#670. $30.00–35.00.

7¾" Golden pheasant.
#1538. $35.00–40.00.

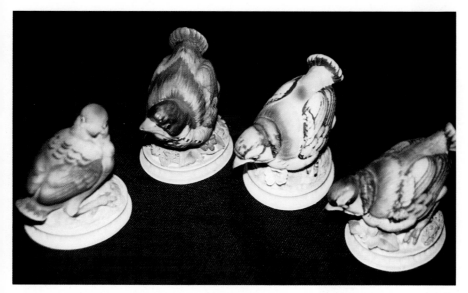

3½" Baby birds.
#1637. $15.00–18.00 each.

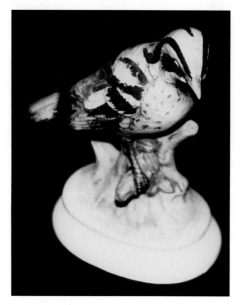

5" Warbler.
#4206. $12.00–15.00.

4" Bobwhite.
#2002. $20.00–25.00.

4½" Hummingbird.
#464. $20.00–24.00.

4¼" Doves.
#2291. $12.00–15.00 each.

6½" Roosters.
#1052. $60.00–70.00 pair.

6½" Roosters.
#1051. $60.00–70.00 pair.

5½" Cats w/rhinestones, matte, set of three.
#3212. $18.00–21.00.

4½" Cardinal.
#464. $20.00–24.00.

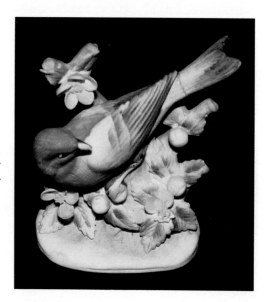

4½" Bluebird.
#464. $20.00–24.00.

6" Roosters
#494. $60.00–70.00 pair.

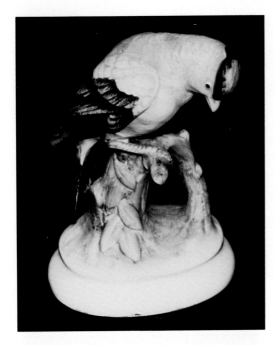

5" Gold Finch.
#395. $15.00–18.00.

5" Parakeet,
#395. $15.00–18.00.

5" Sparrow.
#864. $28.00–32.00.

4½" Owl, bisque.
#121. $17.00–21.00.

9" Rooster and Hen.
#2396. $28.00–32.00.

5½" Pink Flamingo, artistically designed, naturally colored bird with baby flamingo on base.
#504. $65.00–70.00 pair.

3¾" Butterfly on flowers.
#2317. $15.00–18.00.

4¾" Butterfly on floral piece.
#2318. $22.00–28.00.

Boxes

Rose Chinz pin box.
#566. $8.00–12.00.

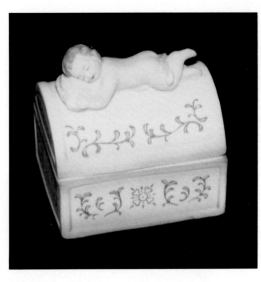

3" Pin box w/baby.
#2710. $10.00–12.00.

3½" Pin box.
#5206. $10.00–12.00.

2" Pin box, antique ivory bisque.
#207. $6.00–8.00.

5" Square candy box.
#4341. $28.00–32.00.

2½" Pin box.
#2151. $22.00–27.00.

5½ Candy box, egg shaped.
#2209. $13.00–17.00.

5" Candy box w/roses, Milk China.
#1192. $45.00–50.00.

7" Covered box, Milk China.
#843. $60.00–70.00.

3" x 5" Candy box.
#2152. $50.00–55.00.

Jewel box w/cover.
#2748. $55.00–65.00.

4" Covered box, antique ivory bisque.
#217. $12.00–15.00.

5½"Candy box, bisque egg shaped.
#2243. $30.00–35.00.

4½" Candy box, egg shaped.
#2204. $8.00–10.00.

2¼" Pin boxes, antique ivory bisque, each.
#642. $6.00–8.00.

2½" Pin box, round.
#2443. $22.00–27.00.

2½" Pin box, heart shaped.
#2443. $22.00–27.00.

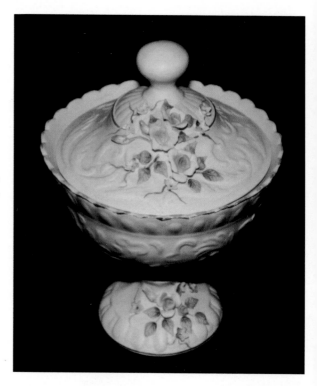

7½" Candy box, ice pink bisque.
#1037. $60.00–70.00.

Pin box in pink with rhinestones.
#90254. $18.00–22.00.

3½" Pin box, round w/birds on top.
#3433. $12.00–15.00.

4" Powder box.
#90092. $40.00–45.00.

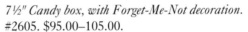

7½" Candy box, with Forget-Me-Not decoration.
#2605. $95.00–105.00.

4¾" Round box.
#308. $17.00–21.00.

Covered candy box, Pear N Apple.
#3766. $15.00–18.00.

Busts of Famous Men

5½" Chopin.
#1166. $18.00–25.00.
7" Liszt.
#2303. $38.00–42.00.
5½" Beethoven.
#1176. $18.00–25.00.
5½" Brahms.
#1161. $18.00–25.00.

5½" Franklin.
#1146. $18.00–25.00.
5½" Bernard Shaw.
#2511. $18.00–25.00.

5½" U.S. Grant.
#2297. $18.00–25.00.
5½" Washington.
#1121. $18.00–25.00.

5½" Charles Dickens.
#2301. $18.00–25.00.
5½" Mark Twain.
#2295. $18.00–25.00.

5½" Lincoln.
#1114. $18.00–25.00.

Canister Sets and Cookie Jars

Pear N Apple, 4 piece cannister set.
#4131. $85.00–95.00.

Fiesta, 4 piece cannister set.
#5254. $80.00–90.00.

10" Cookie jar, Green Orchard.
#3762. $60.00–70.00.

7½" Cookie jar, Miss Priss.
#1502. $105.00–115.00.

7" Cookie jar, Grape.
#3319. $80.00–90.00.

10" Cookie jar, Rustic Daisy.
#3859. $65.00–75.00.

10" Cookie jar, Hot Poppy.
#5399. $45.00–50.00.

12" Cookie jar, Fiesta.
#5256. $40.00–45.00.

9¾" Cookie jar, Chef Girl.
#2360. $70.00–80.00.

11½" Cookie jar, Mushroom Forest.
#6352. $45.00–50.00.

Planter, bloomer girl.
#24. $22.00–27.00.

Salt and pepper, Mr. & Mrs. Claus.
#73. $18.00–22.00.

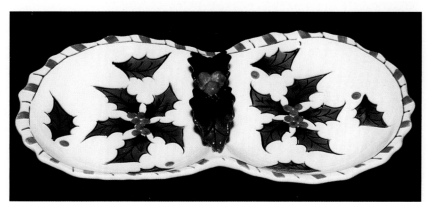

Dish, divided, Holly w/touches of
candy cane red.
#31. $30.00–35.00.

Mug, Christmas, Santa with Mrs. Claus on back.
#868. $20.00–25.00.

Figurine, Candy Cane Kid, 4¼".
#8745. $8.00–10.00.

Sugar and creamer, Holly w/touches of
candy cane red.
#29. $30.00–35.00.

Cup and saucer, Holly w/touches of candy cane red.
#26. $15.00–18.00.

Plate, Holly w/touches of candy cane red.
#2617. $12.00–15.00.

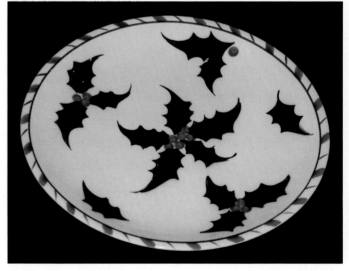

Sugar and creamer, Poinsettia.
#4384. $25.00–30.00.

8½" Coffee pot, 5 cup, Poinsettia.
#4383. $80.00–90.00.

6" Bone dish, Poinsettia.
#4398. $6.00–8.00.

8" Teapot, 6 cup, Poinsettia.
#4388. $80.00–90.00.

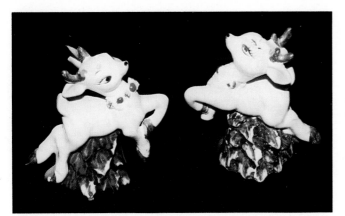

Salt and pepper, Reindeer.
#1477. $15.00–17.00.

Coffee pot, Holly.
#1964. $90.00–110.00.

Sugar and creamer, Holly.
#1965. $40.00–45.00.

7" Nappy dish, Poinsettia.
#4394. $12.00–16.00.

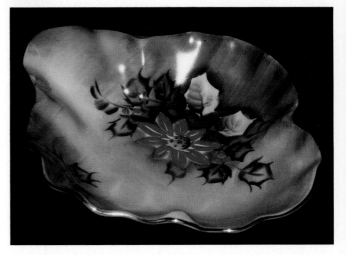

Mug, Green Holly.
#1366. $9.00–11.00.

Coffee pot, 6 cup, Golden Tree.
#1873. $80.00–90.00.

Sugar and creamer, Golden Tree.
#1880. $35.00–40.00.

10½" Cookie jar, winking Santa.
#90148. $150.00–180.00.

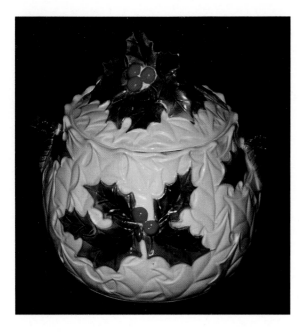

7½" Cookie jar, White Holly.
#6054. $60.00–70.00.

Mr & Mrs. Santa Claus, sitting.
#018. $55.00–60.00.

Jam jar, Holly.
#2039. $40.00–45.00.

2½" Salt and pepper, Poinsettia.
#4390. $15.00–18.00.

Compotes

9" Compote, Brown Heritage, Fruit.
#117. $70.00–80.00.

7" Compote, reticulated w/roses on white.
#109. $25.00–28.00.

Compote w/violets.
#650. $22.00–27.00.

Compotes w/latticed edge, decorated with violets.
#2330. $42.00–48.00.

7¼" Compote.
#713. $12.00–15.00.

7" Compote, white with pink roses.
#712. $15.00–18.00.

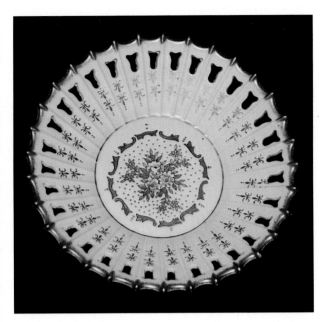

8" Compote, pink latticed.
#2027. $15.00–18.00.

7" Green Heritage.
#2274. $18.00–20.00.

5½" x 8", Forget-Me-Not.
#2604. $95.00–105.00.

Cups and Saucers

Cup and saucer, after dinner.
#1643. $8.00–12.00.

Cup and saucer, jumbo dad, each.
#2595. $22.00–25.00.
Cup and saucer, jumbo mother, each.
#2593. $22.00–25.00.

Cup and saucer, green with floral design, gold trimming.
#801. $25.00–30.00.

5" Cup and saucer, after dinner.
#2421. $20.00–25.00.

Cup and saucer, Festival.
#2616. $10.00–12.00.

Cup and saucer, after dinner, French Rose.
#3450. $8.00–10.00.

Cup and saucer, green, gold, and white.
#546. $25.00–28.00.

Cup and saucer, after dinner, Magnolia.
#2524. $10.00–12.00.
9" Plate, Magnolia.
#2521. $17.00–20.00.

Cup and saucer, turquoise and white.
#801. $25.00–30.00.

Cup and saucer, Brown Heritage, Floral.
#1883. $38.00–42.00.

Cup and saucer, footed white porcelain with rose trim.
#2125. $30.00–35.00.

Cup and saucer, tea, Blue Paisley.
#2133. $18.00–22.00.

Cup and saucer, August, Poppy.
#2829. $15.00–20.00.

Cup and saucer, white w/gold and roses.
#20335. $14.00–18.00.

Cup and saucer, green w/pink roses, pearlized.
#2058. $25.00–30.00.

Cup and saucer, Blue Rose, after dinner.
#2120. $8.00–10.00.

Cup and saucer, tea, Blue Rose.
#1350. $12.00–15.00.

Cup and saucer, Forget-Me-Not.
#4177. $9.00–12.00.

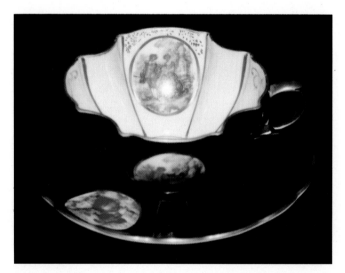

Cup and saucer, tea, black porcelain.
#128. $38.00–42.00.

Cup and saucer, tea, Eastern Star.
#2337. $18.00–22.00.

Cup and saucer, Dogwood design.
#2791. $20.00–25.00.

Cup and saucer, tea, Heirloom Rose.
#1076. $25.00–30.00.

Cup and saucer, tea, Green Heritage.
#3067. $25.00–30.00.

Cup and saucer, Brown Heritage, Fruit.
#561. $38.00–42.00.

Decorative Accessories

3" White Milk China swan.
#846. $18.00–22.00.

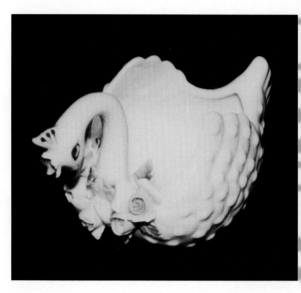

13½" Lamp.
#931. $85.00–95.00.

5" Apothecary jar, Milk China.
#831. $45.00–50.00.

5½" Kerosene lamp, Rose Chintz.
#686. $18.00–22.00.

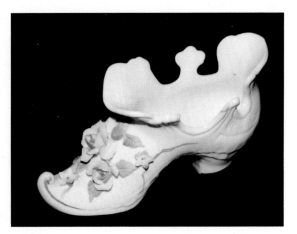

4½" Shoe, white.
#1204. $18.00–22.00.

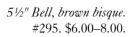

5½" Bell, brown bisque.
#295. $6.00–8.00.

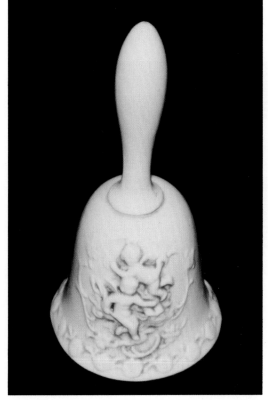

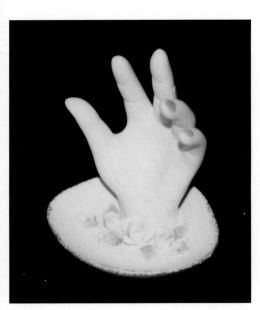

3¾" Ring holder.
#1444. $18.00–22.00.

3 Piece perfume set.
#842. $75.00–85.00.

3¼" Lipstick holder, French Rose.
#3381. $9.00–11.00.

Perfume set, 3 piece, pink with rhinestones.
#90542. $90.00–105.00.

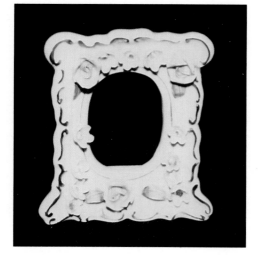

4" Picture frame with roses and rhinestones.
#90511. $16.00–20.00.

6½" Angel lamp, bisque.
#531. $38.00–42.00.

3¼" Ring holder.
#5207. $9.00–11.00.

5½" Swan, white porcelain with all over floral decoration.
#8059. $50.00–55.00.

4" Swan, pink porcelain with all over floral decoration.
#8058. $40.00–45.00.

6" Bookends, Chinese boy and girl, glazed.
#80164. $125.00–140.00.

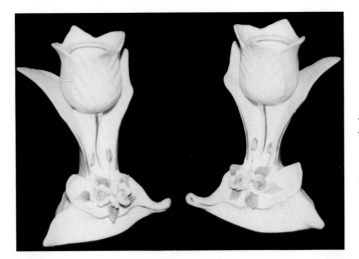

5" Candleholders, bisque.
#2451. $45.00–50.00.

4" Candleholders, Milk China.
#835. $55.00–65.00.

6" x 4" Bird bath candleholder w/angel.
#987. $25.00–30.00.

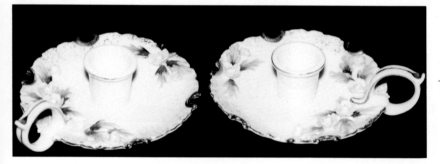

5" Candleholders, white porcelain w/pink and blue flowers.
#9958. $50.00–60.00.

9" Covered candy jar, Forget-Me-Not, trimmed in gold.
#2606. $95.00–105.00.

7" Candy bucket, Forget-Me-Not.
#7297. $35.00–40.00.

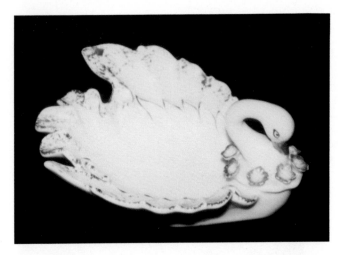

6" White swan candy dish, w/roses and gold.
#954. $40.00–45.00.

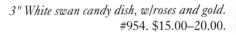

3" White swan candy dish, w/roses and gold.
#954. $15.00–20.00.

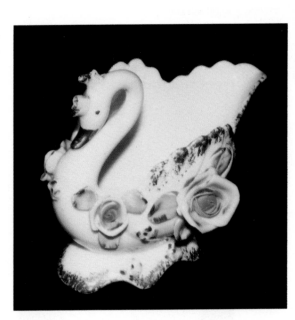

4¼" White china swan bowl, decorated in sponge gold with pink roses.
#721. $65.00–75.00.

5" Candy bucket, w/fruit.
#7364. $35.00–40.00.

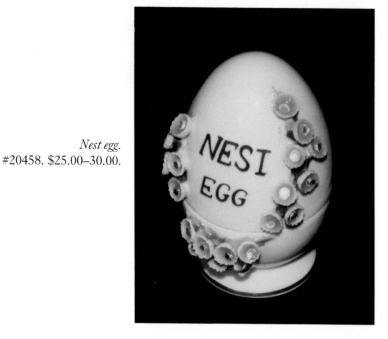

Nest egg.
#20458. $25.00–30.00.

4½" Bird bath.
#6077. $30.00–35.00.

3" Pink china bell with Forget-Me-Not decoration.
#90460. $18.00–22.00.

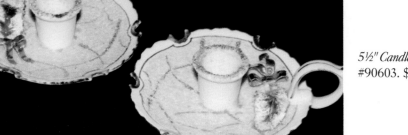

5½" Candleholder w/feather, pink, white, and gold.
#90603. $65.00–70.00.

Figurines

4½" Figurine, matte finish.
#3082. $30.00–40.00.

8½" Provincial boy and girl, pair.
#5968. $80.00–85.00.

5" Provincial boy and girl, pair.
#4243. $40.00–50.00.

5½" Little girl.
#5153. $15.00–20.00.

6" Girl leaning on tree.
#5051. $35.00–45.00.

6" Boy leaning on tree.
#5051. $35.00–45.00.

5" Girl with basket.
#1464. $25.00–30.00.

6" Girl with flowers.
#340. $24.00–28.00.

4¼" Dancing girls, pair.
#392. $28.00–32.00.

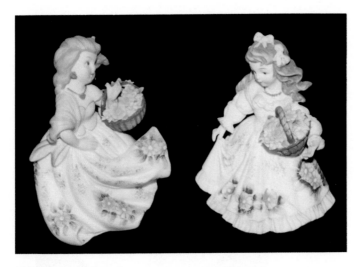

4½" Flower girl, each.
#125. $38.00–42.00.

6¾" Girl with flower basket.
#5050. $25.00–30.00.

7" Bisque girl with basket.
#4047. $50.00–60.00.

10" Colonial woman, "Old Masters."
#341. $50.00–60.00.

7" Colonial girl, bisque.
#3045. $38.00–42.00.

8" Colonial woman.
#344. $60.00–65.00.

6¼" Flower girl.
#335. $40.00–45.00.

8" Colonial lady.
#869. $55.00–65.00.

4¾" Lady in a chair, "Old Masters."
#3826. $25.00–30.00.

5" Girl figurine.
#1700. $35.00–40.00.

6½" Lady figurine.
#1703. $28.00–32.00.

6" Lady.
#5604. $55.00–60.00.

6½" Girl figurine with flowers, each.
#693. $35.00–40.00.

6½" Lady figurine.
#4232. $18.00–22.00.

6" Lady figurine.
#333. $20.00–25.00.

6¼" Lady and man.
#457. $95.00–105.00 pair.

8" Gay Nineties.
#8574. $125.00–135.00 each.

8" China figurines with stippled gold fuzz on white.
#8274. $125.00–135.00 each.

8" Pinkie and blue boy, glazed.
#3049. $70.00–80.00 pair.

4" Bloomer girl.
#3080. $22.00–25.00.

4" Story dolls, beautifully detailed porcelain, figure named on base. #1052. $22.00–28.00 each.

4" Bloomer girls.
#576. $48.00–52.00 each.

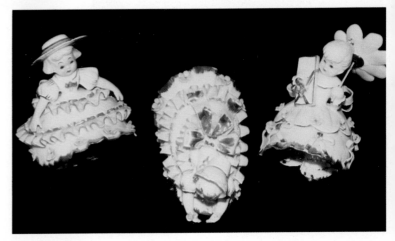

4" Bloomer girls.
#1412. $48.00–52.00 each.

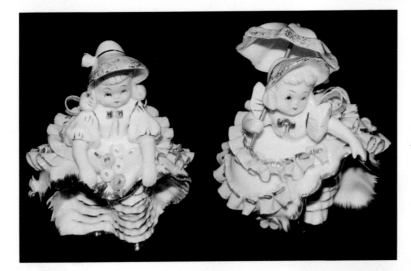

4" Bloomer girls.
#1698. $48.00–52.00 each.

Lady figurines.
#10307. $40.00–45.00 each.

*3½" Unbreakable lace ballerina with five layers of pastel colored lace, applied on bisque china figure.
#707. $40.00–45.00.*

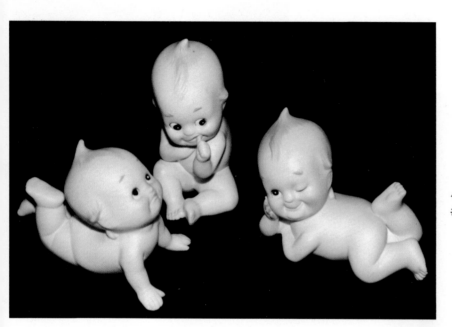

*4½" Bisque Kewpies, 3 poses, each.
#228. $35.00–40.00.*

*5¼" Modern figurines, all white.
#1129. $45.00–50.00 pair.*

*4½" Chinese figurines with rhinestones.
#1999. $28.00–32.00 pair.*

5" Double cupids.
#3642. $13.00–17.00.

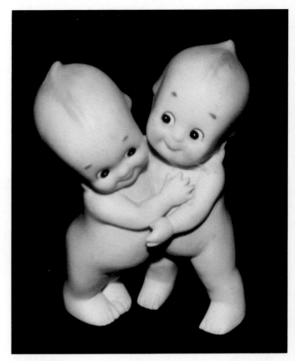

6¾" Man with boy fishing.
#2807. $55.00–65.00.

4½" Girl.
#5154. $18.00–22.00.

7½" Woodcarver with boy.
#5296. $55.00–65.00.

6¼" Lady.
#462. $65.00–75.00.

4½" Figurine with rhinestones.
#10005. $30.00–35.00.

Bloomer girl on stand.
#1234. $28.00–32.00.

Jam Jars

4¼" Mr. Toodles.
#3290. $15.00–18.00.

4" Grape.
#3023. $18.00–22.00.

5½" Green Orchard.
#3745. $10.00–12.00.

4½" Pineapple.
#1071. $9.00–12.00.

4¾" Vineyard.
#3031. $11.00–13.00.

Bluebird.
#436. $30.00–35.00.

5" Della Robbia.
#1958. $8.00–11.00.

Pitchers and Bowls

4" Pitcher with 6½" bowl, floral bisque.
#3221. $25.00–30.00.

8 Cup pitcher, Brown Heritage, Floral.
#3114. $75.00–85.00.

5¼" Pitcher with 7¼" bowl, Forget-Me-Not.
#4189. $28.00–32.00.

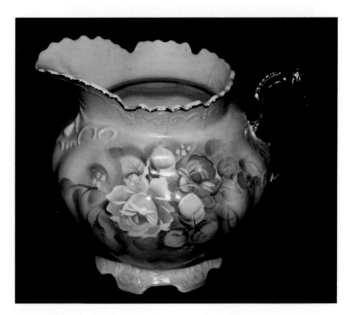

6½" Pitcher, Green Heritage.
#796. $55.00–65.00.

Planters

6" Planter, matte antique ivory.
#384. $25.00–30.00.

5" Planter, antique ivory bisque.
#722. $18.00–20.00 each.
4½" Planter, antique ivory bisque.
#723. $12.00–14.00 each.

3½" Mug planter.
#569. $10.00–12.00.

8" Planter, whiteware.
#2313. $40.00–45.00.

5½" Duck planter.
#905. $30.00–35.00.

3½" Planter, ice pink bisque.
#1183. $28.00–32.00.

6" x 2¾" Jardinaire with roses, Milk China.
#1194. $40.00–45.00.

3" x 4" Planter, whiteware.
#3099. $11.00–13.00.

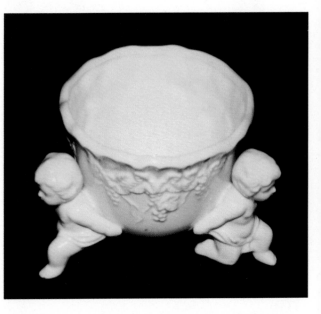

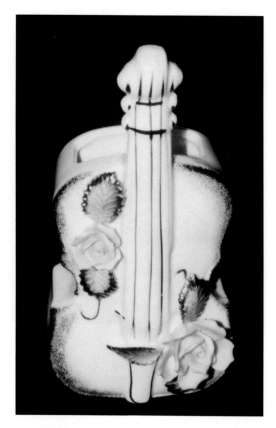

7¼" Planter, violin.
#1734. $15.00–18.00.

7" Girl planter.
#3138. $25.00–28.00.

6" Planter, opening 2½" x 4¼" x 2½".
#167. $12.00–15.00.

4½" x 5½" Planter, matte, elegant white.
#2707. $16.00–20.00.

Bible planter, Ten commandments with lilacs and rhinestones.
#408. $14.00–18.00.

5½" Pheasant planter.
#904. $30.00–35.00.

Planter, angel.
#165. $35.00–40.00.

Planter, bluebird.
#288. $30.00–35.00.

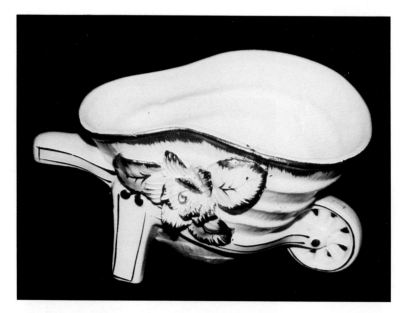

3¾" Planter, white with pale blue grapes.
#2189. $28.00–32.00.

3½" Planter, wheelbarrow, elegant white.
#071. $12.00–15.00.

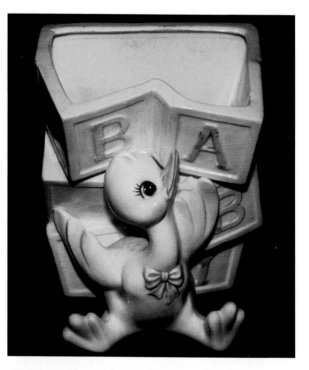

3" Kewpie flower holder.
#1248. $10.00–12.00.

6" Baby planter.
#6365. $12.00–15.00.

Religious

4½" Angel bust, pair.
#1415. $70.00–80.00.

10½" St. Francis with bowl.
#491. $45.00–50.00.

4½" Madonna bust, glazed.
#3207. $15.00–20.00.

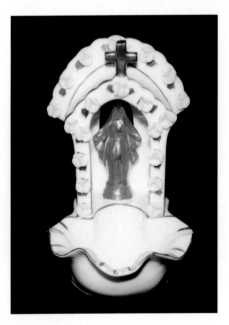

6" Holy Water font, glazed.
#90030. $45.00–50.00.

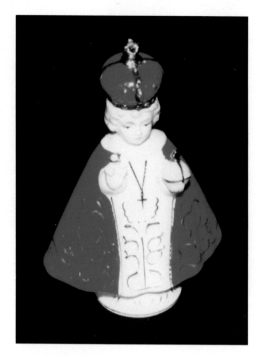

8" Infant of Prague richly decorated in pastel shades.
#718L. $130.00–150.00.
5" Infant of Prague richly decorated in pastel shades.
#718S. $65.00–75.00.

Infant of Prague.
#223. $20.00–25.00.

Madonna bust with beautifuly sculptured hands in prayerful position, pastel tinted in pink and blue. Raised handmade roses on base of figure. Gold halo and trimming.
#433. $80.00–90.00.

7¾" Madonna bust.
#1462. $35.00–40.00.

4½" Angel bust, wall plaques.
#6417. $70.00–80.00 pair.

8" St. Anthony with child.
#8762. $45.00–50.00.

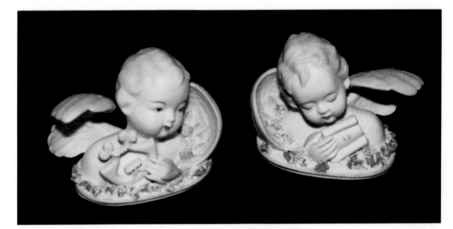

3" Beautiful sleeping and awake cherubs in pastel blue and pink, delicately tinted bisque china.
#432. $80.00–90.00 pair.

4½" Madonna with child in pastel bisque finish.
#237. $70.00–80.00.

7" Madonna with child.
#1416. $70.00–80.00.

8½" Madonna of the flowers in soft pastel bisque.
#1057. $95.00–110.00.

6½" Madonna with child.
#2583. $38.00–42.00.

6" Sacred hearts of Maria and Jesus, each.
#8695 and #8694. $60.00–70.00.

Salt and Pepper Shakers

2¾" Brown Heritage, Floral.
#613. $18.00–22.00.

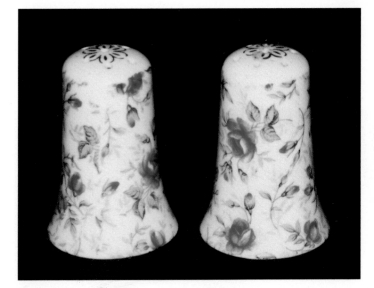

2¾" Rose Chintz.
#665. $15.00–18.00.

2¾" Brown Heritage, Fruit.
#2760. $18.00–22.00.

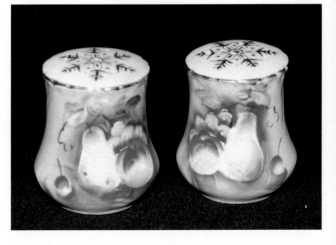

3" Pineapple.
#3053. $25.00–30.00.

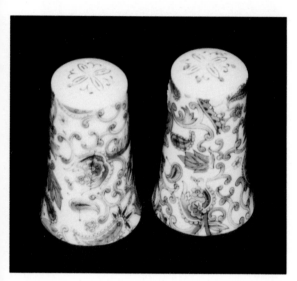

Blue Paisley.
#2346. $8.00–10.00.

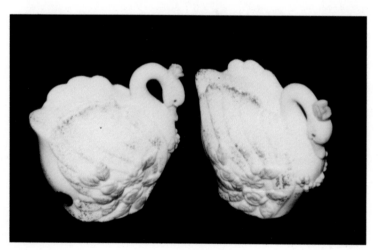

2½" Swans.
#2254. $13.00–17.00.

3" 50th Anniversary.
#1955. $7.00–9.00.

3" 25th Anniversary.
#1957. $7.00–9.00.

3" Dogs with rhinestones for eyes.
#30404. $18.00–22.00.

3" Owls with rhinestones for eyes.
#30145. $18.00–22.00.

3" Rose design.
#676. $12.00–18.00.

2¾" Wheat design.
#30119. $10.00–14.00.

Girl face.
#439. $20.00–25.00.

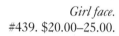

2¾" Cheese and mouse.
#901. $15.00–18.00.

2½" Girl heads.
#1711. $8.00–12.00.

3¾" Mr. Toodles.
#3235. $12.00–15.00.

Comical boy and girl.
#1636. $15.00–18.00.

Forget-Me-Not.
#4184. $7.00–9.00.

Festival.
#2626. $8.00–10.00.

Miss Priss.
#1511. $16.00–18.00.

2¼" Green Heritage.
#3070. $12.00–15.00.

3¼" Rustic Daisy.
#3857. $7.00–11.00.

3¼" Pink Daisy.
#5163. $6.00–8.00.

6½" Hot Poppy.
#5400. $14.00–18.00.

Violets.
#676. $12.00–18.00.

3" Pear N Apple.
#3748. $8.00–12.00.

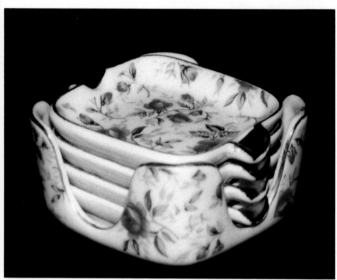

4 Nested ashtrays, Rose Chintz.
#666. $16.00-18.00.

4 Nested ashtrays, Violet Chintz.
#666. $16.00-18.00.

5" White china cigarette holder or flower holder dec-
orated with gold and raised pink flowers.
#929. $50.00-60.00.

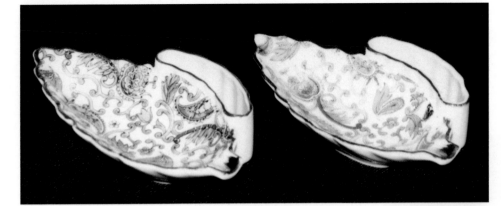

5¼" x 3" Ashtray with urn, Blue Paisley.
#2360. $15.00-20.00 each.

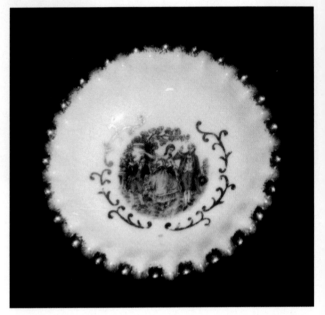

Ashtray, Romance design.
#5418. $6.00-8.00.

4" Cigarette holder.
#1196. $8.00-10.00.

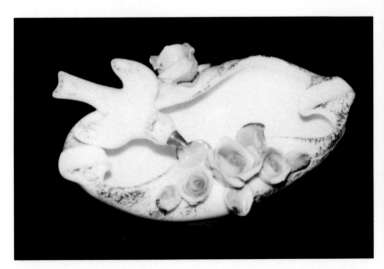

5" Oval white porcelain ashtray with bird.
#262. $25.00-30.00.

3½" Swan ashtray in white with Violet decoration.
#139. $18.00-22.00.

6" Ashtray.
#6964. $10.00-12.00.

Cigarette holder and ashtray, Fleur de Lis.
#1028. $14.00-17.00.

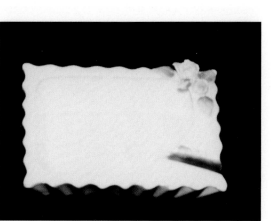

Ashtray, white bisque with roses.
#837. $7.00-9.00.

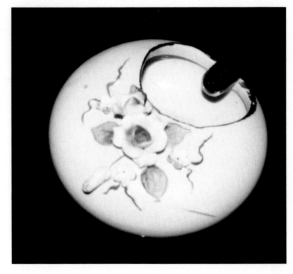

3½" Ashtray, pink bisque w/flowers.
#1501. $8.00-10.00.

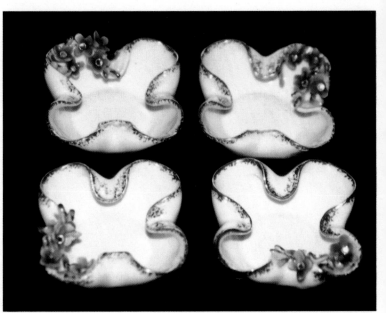

Ashtrays w/lilacs in one corner, set of four.
#194. $32.00-36.00.

3½" Cigarette urn with two ashtrays, pink.
#4700. $75.00-85.00.

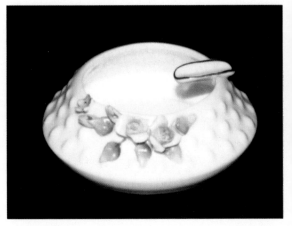

3½" Ashtray, milk china.
#844. $12.00-15.00.

Sugars and Creamers

Festival sugar and creamer.
#2615. $15.00-18.00.

Blue Paisley sugar and creamer,
#2358 with tray, #2351. $15.00-18.00.

Blue Paisley sugar and creamer.
#1974. $18.00-22.00.

2¾" French Rose sugar and creamer.
#4071. $7.00-9.00.

Heirloom Violet sugar and creamer.
#1075. $40.00-45.00.

Violet Chintz sugar and creamer.
#661. $40.00-45.00.

Rose Chintz sugar and creamer.
#661. $40.00-45.00.

Rose Chintz sugar and creamer.
#663. $20.00-25.00.

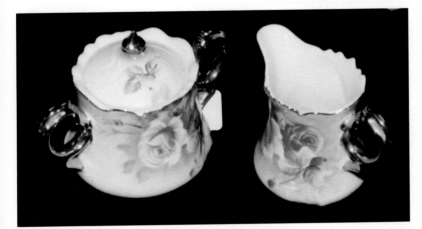

Green Heritage sugar and creamer.
#3066. $42.00-47.00.

4" Magnolia sugar and creamer.
#2520. $25.00-30.00.

Brown Heritage, Floral, sugar and creamer.
#1867. $45.00-50.00.

Brown Heritage, Fruit, sugar and creamer.
#20592. $45.00-50.00.

2½" White bisque, sugar and creamer.
#215. $12.00-15.00.

Wheat design, sugar and creamer.
#20120. $18.00-22.00.

Bluebirds, sugar and creamer.
#290. $35.00-40.00.

Miss Priss, sugar and creamer.
#1508. $35.00–40.00.

Forget-Me-Not, sugar and creamer.
#4175. $22.00–26.00.

Moss Rose, sugar and creamer.
#3167. $28.00–32.00.

Rose, sugar and creamer stacked, decorated in Dresden type roses. #958. $55.00-65.00.

Heirloom Rose, sugar and creamer. #1075. $40.00-45.00.

Mr. Toodles, sugar and creamer. #3292. $25.00-30.00.

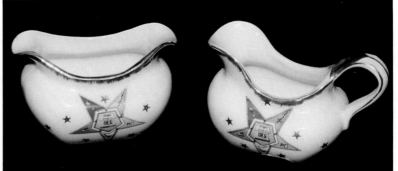

Eastern Star, sugar and creamer.
#2789. $24.00-28.00.

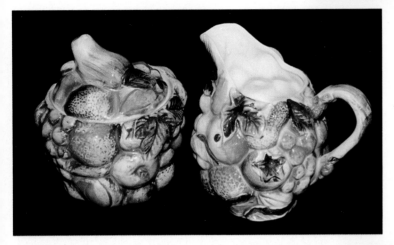

Fruits of Italy, sugar and creamer.
#1177. $12.00-15.00.

Green Orchard, sugar and creamer.
#3744. $14.00-18.00.

Girl head, sugar and creamer.
#1708. $18.00-22.00.

Teapots and Coffee Pots

Combination sugar, creamer, and teapot in a very unique design decorated in lovely Dresden type roses. #985. $125.00–140.00.

Heirloom Violet, teapot. #1075. $90.00–100.00.

Brown Heritage, Fruit, 8 cup coffee pot. #20591. $90.00–100.00.

Brown Heritage, Fruit, 8 cup teapot.
#3113. $90.00–100.00.

Green Heritage, 6 cup teapot.
#792. $75.00–85.00.

8¾" Violet Chintz, coffee pot.
#660. $80.00–90.00.

8¾" Rose Chintz, coffee pot.
#660. $80.00–90.00.

Brown Hertiage, Floral, coffee pot.
#1866. $90.00–100.00.

Magnolia, 5 cup coffee pot.
#2518. $42.00–48.00.

7¼" Festival, teapot.
#2613. $40.00–45.00.

Blue Paisley, 6 cup coffee pot.
#1972. $50.00–60.00.

7¾" Misty Rose, teapot with sugar and creamer.
#5536 & 5537. $40.00–50.00 & $25.00–30.00.

9½" Musical teapot, plays "Tea for Two."
#7543. $35.00–40.00.

Moss Rose, 8 cup coffee pot.
#3166. $45.00–50.00.

Fleur-de-Lis, 5 cup coffee pot.
#2910. $45.00–50.00.

Rose Chintz, teapot, 6 cup.
#911. $80.00–90.00.

Wheat design, teapot.
#20182. $42.00–48.00.

Forget-Me-Not, 6 cup coffee pot.
#4174. $38.00–42.00.

Heirloom Rose, teapot.
#1075. $90.00–100.00.

7" Grape, teapot.
#2663. $35.00–38.00.

Green Heritage, 5 cup coffee pot.
#3065. $75.00–85.00.

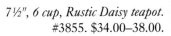

7½", 6 cup, Rustic Daisy teapot.
#3855. $34.00–38.00.

6 Cup, Pear N Apple, teapot.
#3741. $23.00–26.00.

Tea and Toast, Snack Sets

8" Brown Heritage, Floral.
#1864. $18.00–22.00.

9" Fleur-de-Lis.
#1801. $11.00–13.00.

Rose Chintz.
#637. $16.00–18.00.

Violet Chintz.
#638. $16.00–18.00.

8" Green Heritage.
#3071. $15.00–18.00.

9" Lilac Chintz.
#697. $14.00–16.00.

Blue Paisley.
#2340. $11.00–13.00.

8" Forget-Me-Not.
#4179. $12.00–16.00.

8" Wheat design.
#2768. $10.00–12.00.

8" TV snack set, different colors.
#2759. $15.00–18.00.

8" Brown Heritage, Fruit.
#20130. $18.00–22.00.

7" Pitcher vase.
#4209. $22.00–24.00.

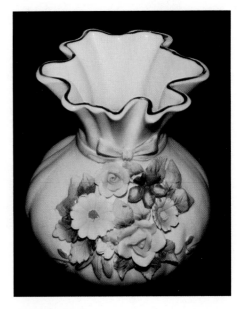

4½" Purse vase.
#4732. $15.00–18.00.

5" Harp shaped vase.
#4739. $15.00–18.00.

6¼" Pitcher vase.
#4540. $15.00–18.00.

4½" Egg shaped vase.
#4342. $9.00–12.00.

5½" Hands vase.
#4198. $18.00–21.00.

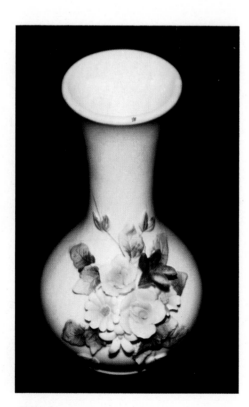

4" Bud vase.
#1847. $13.00–17.00.

7¼" vase.
#1040. $30.00–35.00.

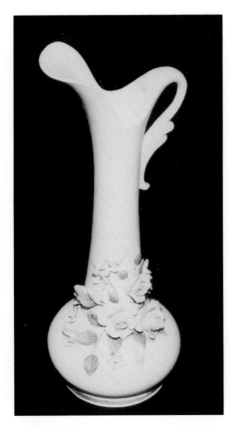

5½" Vase.
#1043. $45.00–50.00.

6" Vase.
#829. $25.00–30.00.

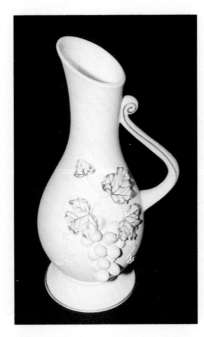

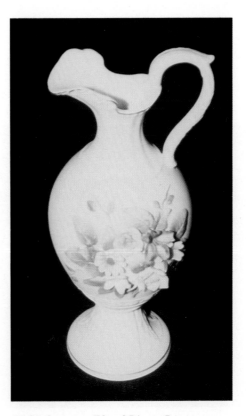

7½" Vase.
#2186. $20.00–25.00.

7" Pitcher vase, Floral Bisque Bouquet.
#4531. $20.00–25.00.

4½" Vase, Lilac.
#2940. $27.00–30.00.

7" Vase, Lilac.
#2942. $27.00–30.00.

3" Heart flower holder, ivory bisque.
#1817. $7.00–10.00.

4" Porcelain miniature vase, Forget-Me-Not
trim.
#7086. $22.00–26.00.

8¾" vase, Brown Heritage, Floral.
#3116. $32.00–37.00.

5½" Vase, Brown Heritage, Floral.
#2763. $15.00–18.00.

8" Flower vase, Milk China.
#832. $70.00–80.00.

6" Vase, Lilac with rhinestones.
#393. $70.00–75.00.

123

5" Pineapple vase.
#7283. $60.00–70.00.

6½" Lady head vase.
#GZL. $35.00–40.00.

Fluted bag vase in pink porclain, gold stippled sandy edge and forget-me-not trimmed in pastel colors.
#7290. $32.00–38.00.

6¼" Fan vase, Milk China.
#840. $70.00–80.00.

7" Hands vase.
#1791. $30.00–35.00.

4" Bud vase, white bisque, with applied flowers.
#1847. $13.00–17.00.

6¼" Vase with pinecones.
#2460. $23.00–27.00 each.

6¼" Pink vase, Forget-Me-Not trim.
#7075. $50.00–55.00.

4" Bud vase, pink bisque, with applied flowers.
#1847. $13.00–17.00.

6" White vase, with violets and rhinestones.
#152. $40.00–45.00.

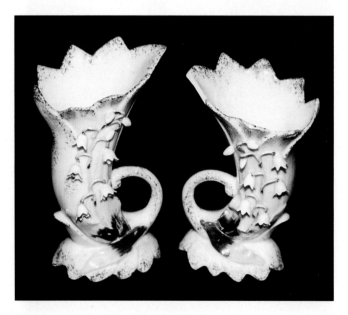

5½" Cornucopia, Lily of the Valley, pair.
#283. $60.00–70.00.

6" Vase with pink roses and ribbons.
#70039. $55.00–65.00.

6¼" Vase, Milk China with roses.
#1189. $50.00–55.00.

7" Vase with Forget-Me-Not trim.
#7295. $80.00–90.00.

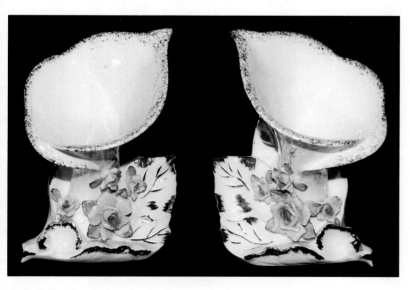

Calla Lily shaped with pink roses, pair.
#7093. $115.00–135.00.

6" Vase, white bisque.
#1044. $65.00–75.00.

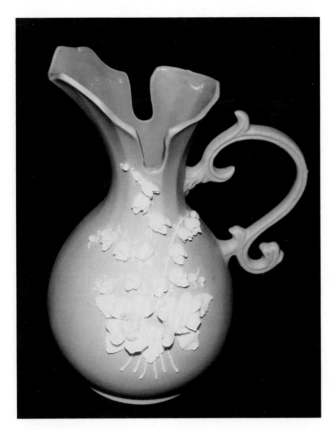

6" Blue bisque vase.
#2178. $25.00–28.00.

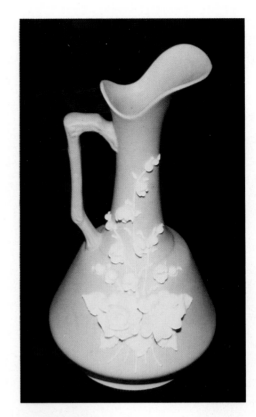

5¾" Blue bisque vase.
#2193. $25.00–28.00.

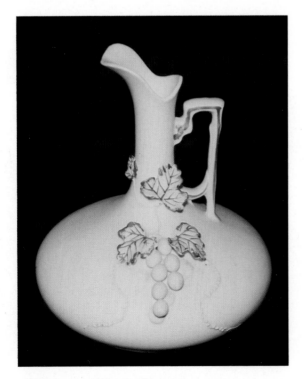

6" White vase with pale blue grapes.
#2187. $27.00–30.00.

10" Ewer type vase with pale blue grapes.
#2456. $35.00–40.00.

7¼" Ewer type vase, Ivory Cameo.
#1875. $22.00–25.00.

7½" Vase with applied fruit.
#7363. $45.00–50.00.

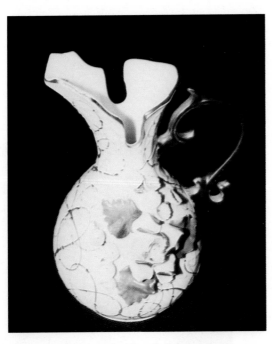

6" Ewer type vase w/gold and pink spaghetti.
#70443. $50.00–55.00.

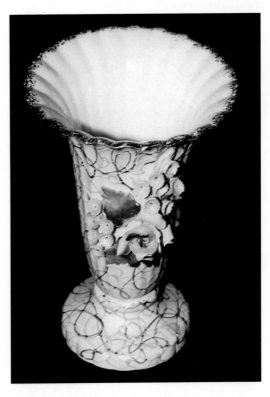

6¾" Vase w/gold and pink spaghetti.
#70444. $60.00–65.00.

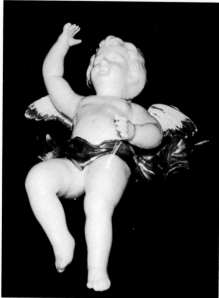

7¼" Angel.
#2371. $30.00–35.00.

7¾" "To Mother" with roses.
#508. $18.00–22.00.

7" Wall pocket "Home Sweet Home."
#219. $15.00–20.00.

4" Plaque, bisque finish.
#820. $12.00–15.00.

8" Wall plaque, Floral, set of four, matte.
#2780. $42.00–48.00.

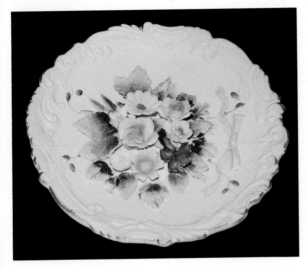

6" Round shaped.
#4743. $14.00–18.00.

8" Floral wall plaque.
#6350. $18.00–22.00.

6" Angel wall plaque, bisque.
#1697. $25.00–30.00.

6½" Wall plaque.
#2147. $25.00–30.00.

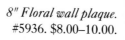

8" Floral wall plaque.
#5936. $8.00–10.00.

8" Flower wall plaques.
#5789. $14.00–18.00 each.

6¼" Wall plaque, colonial girl.
#117. $12.00–15.00.

4½" Wall plaque, angel bust, pair.
#6417. $70.00–80.00.

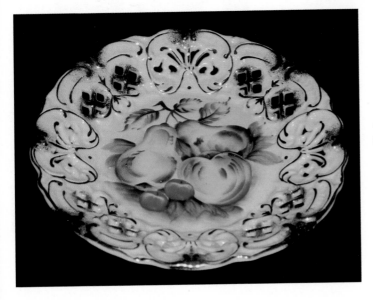

8" Fruit wall plaque.
#268. $15.00–18.00.

8" Floral wall plaque, hand painted.
#119. $18.00–20.00.

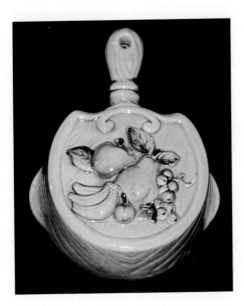

7¼" Pear N Apple wallpocket.
#3850. $10.00–12.00.

4" Lord's Prayer.
#6961. $14.00–18.00.

Robin on branch.
#855. $28.00–32.00.

8" Plate with Lord's Prayer.
#6348. $14.00–17.00.

8" Fruit wall plaque, hand painted.
#119. $18.00–22.00.

Miscellaneous Items

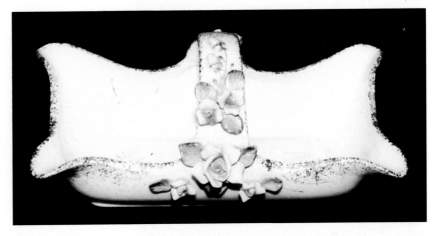

6" Pink porcelain candy basket, raised rose trim.
#2085. $45.00–50.00.

6½" Pink china double hand dish decorated
with pink roses.
#714. $60.00–65.00.

Candy dish, Misty Rose.
#5517. $10.00–12.00.

6½" Leaf nappy, Misty Rose.
#5724. $8.00–10.00.

6" Lemon dish, Magnolia.
#2618. $10.00–15.00.

3½" Coaster, Festival.
#2630. $3.00–5.00.

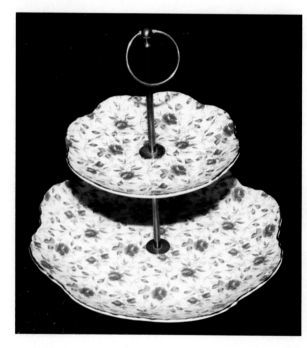

2 Tier tidbit tray, Rose Chintz.
#649 $50.00–60.00.

4½" Teabag holder.
#6672. $7.00–9.00.

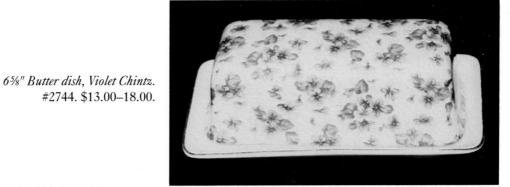

6⅝" Butter dish, Violet Chintz.
#2744. $13.00–18.00.

3" Egg cup, Violet Chintz, each.
#664. $12.00–15.00.

7½" Butter dish, Pear N Apple.
#3739. $12.00–15.00.

5" x 5" Dish, white china with gold and pink
roses for decoration.
#938. $52.00–55.00.

2½" Shell tray.
#841. $15.00–18.00.

Double bonbon.
#366. $28.00–32.00.

8" Dish, pink with gold and floral design.
#3153. $15.00–18.00.

7¼" Cake plate, Green Heritage.
#719. $20.00–25.00.

9¼" Plate, 50th Anniversary.
#3696. $13.00–17.00.

Bonbon dish, Fruit design.
#20127. $22.00–26.00.

9" Plate, Forget-Me-Not.
#4181. $15.00–20.00.

6" Nappy dish, Forget-Me-Not.
#4187. $10.00–12.00.

2 Tier tidbit, Forget-Me-Not.
#4182. $32.00–38.00.

Single tidbit, rose.
#651. $14.00–18.00.

8½" Double bonbon, pink.
#20032. $55.00–60.00.

8" Double dish, wheat design.
#20197. $30.00–35.00.

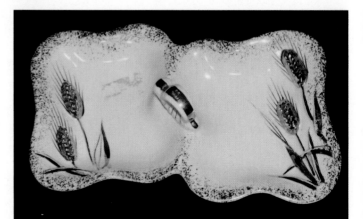

Console set, 3 piece with pink roses.
#721. $75.00–80.00.

7 Piece cake set, Fruit.
#1133. $110.00–135.00.

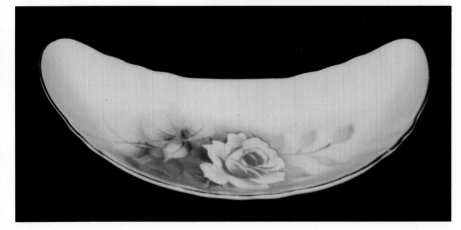

6" Bone dish, Green Heritage.
#3708. $12.00–15.00.

6" Tidbit, Blue Paisley.
#2348. $8.00–12.00.

7½" Plate, dogwood design.
#2818. $18.00–22.00.

3" Mug, 6¼" bowl, 7" plate, baby set.
#2706. $28.00–32.00.

9¾" 2 Compartment dish, Americana.
#938. $38.00–42.00.

Baby set, Bluebirds.
#435 & #284. $40.00–45.00.

2 Tier tidbit tray, Green Heritage.
#1153. $40.00–45.00.

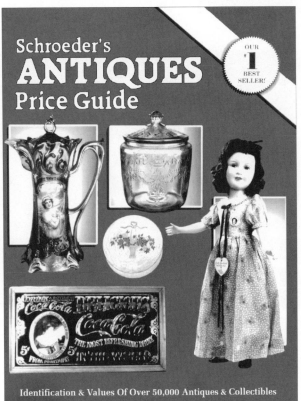